DETOUR to the light

staying positive during life's roadblocks

Wendy Whiting

CFI BOOKS

An Imprint of Cedar Fort, Inc.
Springville, Utah

© 2017 Wendy Whiting
All rights reserved.

No part of this book may be reproduced in any form whatsoever, whether by graphic, visual, electronic, film, microfilm, tape recording, or any other means, without prior written permission of the publisher, except in the case of brief passages embodied in critical reviews and articles.

The opinions and views expressed herein belong solely to the author and do not necessarily represent the opinions or views of Cedar Fort, Inc. Permission for the use of sources, graphics, and photos is also solely the responsibility of the author.

Published by CFI Books, an imprint of Cedar Fort, Inc.
2373 W. 700 S., Springville, UT 84663
Distributed by Cedar Fort, Inc., www.cedarfort.com

Cover design by Kinsey Beckett
Cover design © 2017 Cedar Fort, Inc.
Edited and typeset by Sydnee Hyer

Dedicated to my nieces and nephews: Lillie, Abby, Holly, Ambyr, Landon, Nolan, Emily, Veronika, Zack, and Casey.

Thanks to my parents, siblings, and aunt for being the biggest supporters of my dreams and always reminding me that I can do great things.

"If we approach adversities wisely,
our hardest times can be times of greatest growth, which in turn can lead toward times of greatest happiness."

~ Joseph B. Wirthlin

CONTENTS

Introduction 1
Roadblock One: Depression 3
Detour One: Speak Up 9
Detour Two: Get Up and Get Moving 11
Roadblock Two: Cancer 13
Detour Three: Service 19
Detour Four: Study the Scriptures 22
Roadblock Three: Job Loss 25
Detour Five: Be Grateful 29
Detour Six: Have Hope and Be Positive 31
Roadblock Four: Anxiety Crash 35
Detour Seven: Seek Help 39
Detour Eight: Pray Often and Earnestly 41
Never Give Up 45
Conclusion 49
Bibliography 53
About the Author 55

INTRODUCTION

Neal A. Maxwell wrote, "Merely knowing that some have prevailed is vital in a society filled with 'give-up-itis.'" When I was a teenager, all I wanted was to hear someone's story of how they made it through tough trials like I was going through. I wanted to know someone had actually made it through these trials, and not only made it through but found joy again. I had faith in Heavenly Father's plan for me, but I did not know how I would find joy and normalcy again. The world and possibly some of your friends may tell you how they think you should respond to hard situations, but their solutions do not follow what the gospel teaches. Sometimes those worldly answers will sound good at that moment, but I guarantee you they will not bring lasting happiness. I chose to put the gospel to the test as I faced challenges as a teenager and I am glad I did. It might have been hard, but I gained a testimony from truly relying on my Heavenly Father during the times I thought I could not make it one more day.

I am choosing to share with you my personal stories so that you may have the opportunity to see that choosing the gospel path is worth every sacrifice that comes. I also want to assure you that good times are ahead of you and good things do come again.

I want to present to you four experiences that I had that I thought were major roadblocks on my path through life. At each of these times, I thought I was stuck and I could not see how I could possibly get around these problems. However, I learned that the principles I had learned in church could help me through those times. So after each experience I share with you, I will also give two of the principles that helped me find a detour around that roadblock and gave me stepping blocks to better handle the next trial. But I didn't want you just to hear from me about how to choose the better detour. I have included lots of quotes from influential leaders and some from a few of my great friends who have also faced some of the similar issues you and I have come across.

Above all else I hope this book gives you hope and lets you know that you are not alone. People have been through what you are going through before and if nothing else seems to come close to helping, know that your Father in Heaven loves you and can help you through these tests if you can but come unto Him.

Through Him there is safety and peace.

ROADBLOCK ONE: DEPRESSION

I have always had a very close relationship with my three older brothers. In my teenage years, they were my best friends. I hung out with them all the time and went everywhere with them. So when two of my brothers got married within three months of each other while my third brother was on a mission, I basically freaked out. I was turning sixteen and my life was in a whirlwind. I liked my new sisters-in-law, but in my mind they were taking away my brothers. I figured I would never have the same relationship with them ever again. Somehow them making their own families made me feel like they no longer wanted to be a part of mine. It seemed like a lost cause, because they would not have time to hang out with me or have the place in their hearts to love me too. I figured my brothers would probably move away, forget about me, and move on with their new happy lives without me. Looking back now, those feelings seem a bit dramatic, but back then, it felt like my life was being derailed, and while it may have been dramatic, those feelings were real to me.

I know my sisters-in-law tried to show me they wanted to be friends and I tried to act like I was their friend. It must have been quite confusing to them when I never completely warmed up to them. I had always pictured in my mind that when my brothers got married, life would be so fun and I would finally have sisters. Life would be perfect. Unfortunately, I was too scared of the horrible outcome I just knew would eventually happen to let life work out that way.

    I fell into depression. My brothers were leaving me alone at home with my parents. I was struggling with AP chemistry in school. I spent most of my time that year in my brothers' empty room, studying chemistry and wallowing in my misery. That room was like my prison cell. I was bound to the never-ending homework that I could not comprehend. I was torturing myself staying in that room for hours thinking about how bad I thought things were and how I could not see a bright future ahead. Family was everything and now mine was torn apart, or so I thought.

    All I wanted was someone to approach me and ask me what was wrong. No one ever asked me what was wrong. How could they not see my sorrow? I felt pitiful. I was always a very expressive person, so why could they not see my sadness? My family tried to throw me a surprise birthday party, they tried to do things I liked with me, and they tried to include me in things. But I never saw those as advances in trying to help. I wanted to talk, and all I wanted was someone to ask what was wrong. I prayed every day and night that I would find a way out of this mental torture. Satan was getting me to believe all kinds of horrible things about myself. I prayed that someone would just ask me what was wrong and I could finally unload.

    I look back now and realize that there were opportunities for me to talk to others. I had prayed but somehow I thought I did not have to do the hard work. I thought someone else had to go out of their way to fix my problem. The real issue was that I did not know how to get out of the mess I was in. I read my scriptures every day and said my prayers. I thought that alone was enough to get me out. Those are great things that help us daily, but those two things alone cannot cure our problems. Heavenly Father has given us many more amazing tools to get us out of these types of situations. One of those tools He gave us was our parents, siblings, and other family and friends. It was by turning to them that I eventually figured my way out of my depression.

My mother eventually got me to tell her what was wrong. My poor mother knew I was suffering but did not know how to get me to talk. I had to realize that the only way I was going to get out of this pit of despair was to take that step and talk. My mom wanted to get me help with a doctor. I probably could have used medical help, but I was determined to get out of my pit without a doctor. I thought that if I prayed enough I would get out of this mess. I was missing the principle of acting on my faith. I so wish that I had gone to a professional because I would have been able to see, understand, and conquer my fears so much better. I do not think I knew how to best help myself.

Two things happened in my life that hit me into finally realizing I needed to get out of this depression before I was consumed completely. The first thing that helped me take a step was a party I went to. I hung out with my friends from church and we had a big karaoke party at a leader's house. I had so much fun that I did not feel horrible that night. Nights had always been my worst and loneliest times. I realized that when I had started feeling horrible for myself, I had stopped hanging out with my friends and I stopped having fun. The first key to me climbing out of my pit was to commit myself to not spend so much time by myself and to make sure I had fun. "Men are that they might have joy." That scripture is so easily recited, but the meaning so easily forgotten. We are here in this life to be tried, but we are also here to enjoy the immense amount of gifts the Lord can bless us with.

I was well on my way to taking action in my life. I was writing my brother on a mission constantly and asking for uplifting advice, which he provided weekly. I was actively trying to improve my relationships with my sisters-in-law and my brothers. I was even trying to get out more often and not hide in that cave of a spare room. Life was still hard, but I had hope. Hope made all the difference. There had been a talk one of my married brothers showed me that helped me through almost every trial, but this one especially. The talk was from Elder Jeffrey R. Holland in the October 1999 session of general conference. The talk is entitled, "An High Priest of Good Things to

Come." There is one part of the talk that I printed out and stuck to my bathroom mirror, and all these years later it is still in my bathroom. It reads,

"There is help. There is happiness. There really is light at the end of the tunnel. It is the Light of the World, the Bright and Morning Star, the "light that is endless, that can never be darkened." It is the very Son of God Himself. In loving praise far beyond Romeo's reach, we say, "What light through yonder window breaks?" It is the return of hope, and Jesus is the Sun. To any who may be struggling to see that light and find that hope, I say: Hold on. Keep trying. God loves you. Things will improve. Christ comes to you in His "more excellent ministry" with a future of "better promises." He is your "high priest of good things to come."

This quote helped me to feel like there was hope and that I could make it. If I just held on and kept trying, good things would come again.

As I mentioned earlier, there was one more thing that startled me out of my depression. I was acting and trying to take steps on my own. Then a few weeks after my epiphany of needing to get out of the house more, an acquaintance of mine at school committed suicide. I was horrified. I never found out from a direct source the reason for his actions, but from what I heard he felt trapped. He feared that an action he had taken would get him in deep trouble and in a moment of fear, he ended his life. When I was told how he felt before his death I remember thinking, how could anyone ever think that there was no way out of a mess and that death was the only answer? We were young; how could death ever be the answer? It was like a slap in the face the second I realized I had felt that same despair of not knowing how things could get better. But I had something he didn't. I knew that death was not the answer, but that faith in God was. I felt so sad that he did not know that. It was at that moment that I realized I had a lot of hope. I had lots of people around me who loved and supported me. I had a life, and it was by no means ending soon just because I could not foresee when things would get better. Great things could come again, even if I did not know how. The Lord has a way of showing us He has a plan. Oftentimes we think life will or should go one way and we are upset when it doesn't, but the Lord has a plan that is so much better than we could ever come up with.

    I did not instantly jump out of my depression. I worked on myself and my relationships constantly to improve my situation. I had soul-bearing conversations with my siblings that helped me realize that just because my brothers did not live at my house did not mean I could not have a great relationship with them. I was going to need my own life as I grew up, but no matter where my family was, they were going to be there for me. Over time I saw how my sisters-in-law made my life better and how my future was full of great things to come. In fact, I know I needed those women that married my brothers in my life. My sisters-in-law are now some of my best friends. Funny how something that I was convinced would ruin my life as I knew it really opened up a wonderful world I had never known.

DETOUR ONE: SPEAK UP

The Lord has shown me over and over again that it is through others that He often presents the bit of hope or inspiration we need. I had amazing friends, teachers, parents, siblings, and other family members that gave me the encouragement I needed once I learned to speak up when something was wrong.

President Spencer W. Kimball said, "God does notice us, and he watches over us. But it is usually through another person that he meets our needs. Therefore, it is vital that we serve each other."

Not only is it important that we speak up when we need it but it is important that we be there for our friends and family when they need to be heard. People often have a hard time speaking up. Think about it, if you had a friend who had a problem burning inside or just needed a shoulder for support, wouldn't you put everything aside to help them? Do you think there are people in your life that would do that same thing for you? I am 100% positive that there are, but you might not realize it because the hard part of opening up is realizing that you are not the only one who has or ever will face your current problem. I promise you that the Lord puts people in your path that have a unique perspective and very specific experiences that will be exactly what you need to relate to in order to get through your trials. That might sound like a crazy promise, but I have seen it happen over and over again. I have had trying times in my life when a friend is there to comfort me and they bring up an experience that fits exactly what I needed to hear right then. It is in those times I know God has brought that friend to me to help me in that hard time.

President Henry B. Eyring said,

"All of us will be tested. And all of us need true friends to love us, to listen to us, to show us the way, and to testify of truth to us so that we may retain the companionship of the Holy Ghost. You must be such a true friend."

I challenge you to not only find and open up to such a friend but to also become one. Your experiences right now or in the past might just be what someone else needs to hear. Perhaps the trick you have found to help you through a time of crisis is exactly the trick that another person needs in their life. We can have friends enter our lives to make us better and we can do the same for others.

To learn how powerful a friend or family member can be or how life changing you can be to them watch the video attached to the link below.

https://youtu.be/rIxttI8tN1I

SURVEY SAYS

How do you generally know you need to seek out help?

"When I get extra moody or short with those around me is when I know something isn't quite right. I will do or say something and then my inner voice will say, "Hey, did you really just do/say that?" - Sandy

"When I become so depressed that the normal things that make me happy don't make a difference and I can't snap myself out of it, I know I need help."-Laurie

"When I start thinking bad thoughts about myself or feeling like I can never make things right, I know Satan is on the attack. I have learned that one of the quickest ways to bring back the positive thoughts is to pray and text a friend who is encouraging." - Brian

Who do you like to go to when you need to seek out help?

"First, I pray for help and then I try going to my mom or my closest friends."- Laurie

"I usually go to my mother first. I know she has gone through most of the same trials as I have. She is great at encouraging me." - Jennifer

DETOUR TWO: GET UP AND GET MOVING

Have you ever had nothing to do at all? Maybe in the summer when all your friends seem to be gone and all the TV shows are reruns? You feel useless and like a bump on a log. Humans need to feel productive and to be active. Proverbs 19:15 says, "Slothfulness casteth into a deep sleep; and an idle soul shall suffer hunger."

Elder Neal A. Maxwell wrote,

To draw into our private sanctuaries not only deprives others of our love, our talents, and our service, but it also deprives us of chances to serve, to love, and to be loved.

I do not know about you, but I like being loved and feeling that great feeling I get after I have accomplished something. However, I have felt the opposite too. Satan can easily tempt me to passively let days go by without doing anything at all. The feelings and consequences that come from those days are negative and self-destructive. When we are lazy, grumpiness and the loss of motivation set in. I know I typically start feeling negative about myself and lose hope of things getting better when I am idle.

The best way to break out of the degrading lazy feeling is to do something. Get up and get moving! Be social, improve your talents, learn a new sport, go on a walk, do service, set goals and complete them, or create an art project. These items might sound pretty basic, but they can turn your frown upside down as well as open doors to a better life. It is during times when I am feeling down but force myself to get up and be active that I find things I never knew I loved.

Another great way to get up and do something good is to work on your Personal Progress program or Duty to God program. I was about ready to start my freshman year of high school when I visited my aunt's home in California for the first time. I was there for a week and somehow found a lot of time for reflection. I was sort of an overachiever at times, or more like I liked to cram a lot of hard work in at once so that I could enjoy the benefits later. It was during this vacation that I decided to knock out my Personal Progress. I decided which goals and projects I was going to do and what it would take for me to get my Young Women's medallion. I focused on the scripture-based goals at that time and decided to tackle those first. It was that week that I started my daily scripture reading habit that is still intact today. Had I not increased my spiritual experiences by focusing on my Personal Progress that year, I would not have developed the testimony that helped me to get through the trials that were to come. I finished the program and received my medallion a little over a year later. I am so grateful I took that action right then. I thought I was going to get myself ahead so I wouldn't have to work later, but instead I prepared myself for the spiritual, emotional, and physical whirlwinds ahead.

I also suggest finding and relying on good friends to be social with. It was through being social that I eventually figured out that I was making my depression worse by sitting alone in a room night after night. I have set up rules in my life ever since that experience with depression. I have set limits and tried to be more aware of when I need to get out and do something fun. Friends can help uplift you with encouraging words and by making you laugh. Laughter really is the best medicine. Laughter can take away so much of our grief and stress in a matter of seconds.

ROADBLOCK TWO: CANCER

A couple weeks after my 17th birthday, my mom picked me up from school and told me about my dad's doctor visit. She told me that he had felt something weird in his mouth and had gone to the doctor to see what it was. After some tests were taken, the doctor told my dad that it was possibly cancer but that they would have to wait a week to know for sure. My mom warned me that it might be cancer, but might not. She did not want me to worry, but she thought I should know. From the moment my mom told me, I knew my dad had cancer. I spent the next week trying to do normal things with my friends. I remember going to an ice rink after homecoming that weekend, and because I had a badly sprained ankle, I just sat and watched everyone skate. Several people wanted me to come do something with them, but I wanted to sit and watch the skaters. I think that I needed that time to reflect and find peace. I knew that the following week peace would not come so easily, so I just wanted to soak it in while I could.

Days before his 50th birthday, my dad was diagnosed with malignant neoplasm of the tongue. My family spent the whole night talking about what was going to happen. We discussed how my dad was going to have surgery and that the doctors were pretty sure they would be able to remove it all. I stayed up late just talking and getting used to the idea of my dad having cancer.

When I went to school the next day and took my PSAT, I was more or less in a stupor. After the test, I went to Spanish class and realized that I had never studied for my Spanish test after finding out about my dad's cancer. I went to my teacher and asked if I could take the test later. My teacher gave me a stern look and asked why I should have that privilege, while insisting it would not be fair. I burst into tears. And I am not a person who cries in public. When I was younger my brothers told me over and over again there was no crying in the Whiting house, which made me not want to cry in front of others, so the fact that I cried like this in public was a big shocker to me. The magnitude of the situation hit at that moment and I could not calm down. I got the words out of my mouth that my dad had cancer and I just could not study. She gave me a hug and a hall pass so I could walk off my tears. I went to my locker, stuck my head in, and bawled my eyes out while shaking tremendously. I soon calmed down and walked to the newspaper room. I was on the newspaper staff and knew I could go in there and not be harassed about not being in class. My newspaper teacher and his aide never questioned my reasons for being there and never asked me why I had obviously just been crying. I had a place I could run to and teachers willing to support me.

Conveniently, parent teacher conferences were around the corner at that time. My Spanish teacher expressed her concerns as she told my parents what had happened the day I broke down in class. My dad gave me a blessing, and from that second on, though times were still hard and nerve-racking, I knew that things would work out fine and would be what Heavenly Father planned for me, no matter what happened. My dad also got a blessing from our bishop the night before his surgery and it was of great comfort to my family. The blessings of the priesthood helped us all so much in that time. I felt the presence of the Holy Spirit with me all through those next few months.

The day of my dad's surgery came. My dad woke me up and said goodbye as he gave me a hug. I look back at that moment now and cry because I had no idea that that would be the last time I heard my dad speak as he had in my childhood. I'm so grateful that I had the Spirit's constant watch so I did not contemplate the scariness of the situation.

That day I went to school and took the state standardized retest just to try and get a better score than what I had the year before. I do not know why I wasted my time going at all because all I did was wonder what was going on with my father. As soon as I finished my test, I knew I could not sit in school worrying any longer. My brother signed me out of school and brought me home. My close friend Blanca, who was like a sister to me, came over to be with me. She helped me finish my homework and then took me to the dollar store to buy some stuff for my dad. We bought things for him to do in the hospital and for him to be able to communicate with us through writing. Blanca then took me to the hospital to see my family.

When I got to the hospital, I found out that my father was still in surgery. In total he had been in surgery eight hours. The surgery was supposed to have been maybe about three hours. Everyone was anxious. My dad came out of surgery not too long after I got there. My mom was crying at the thought of telling me how things were. Dad was expected to only have a few spots of cancer but they had to keep sending biopsies back to the lab. The doctors removed two thirds of his tongue. The worst part was that not all the cancer had been removed. The cancer had spread throughout his mouth. My father would need to have chemotherapy and radiation. To make things even worse, he had to have a tracheotomy and a feeding tube put in. I have heard of people using the expression that their heart sank. I always thought it was just figurative, but I felt something hit the bottom of my stomach when I heard the news, and from the way I was feeling, it had to have been my heart. I found comfort when I reminded myself of what was said in my blessing and my father's.

When I walked into that hospital I had no intention of seeing my dad that day. In fact, I told him before his surgery not to expect me to visit while he was at the hospital. I had not wanted to see my dad hooked up to tubes in the ICU. But because of Blanca's encouragement, I went in and saw him with her by my side. It was scary. I did not know what all the tubes did, but I saw blood in one and I did not know how to react. I do not do well with these types of environments so it is no shock that I could not stay long. I had not wanted to visit him in fear that I would remember him that way or that it would be too much. But what I really learned that day was that friendship can provide a support that makes us capable of things far beyond what we feel is possible. I could not have gone in that room without Blanca. I do not think seeing my dad after surgery changed my life, but remembering that Blanca was there holding my hand is a precious memory I will never forget. It was an example of true friendship that showed me what a friend does during difficult times.

Another thing I learned the day of my dad's surgery and the days following is that God gives us small miracles to help us make it through. When my mom and I went home that first night we were greeted by my sister-in-law and niece. My niece, Lillie, had been born earlier that year, and if you ask any member of my family, they will tell you she was a special gift from God to help us during this difficult time. Lillie had a smiley and loving demeanor. She could brighten up a room like no child I had ever seen. After arriving home from the hospital, seeing that little girl's smile reminded me that Heavenly Father had a bigger plan for us. She made me feel like life would still go on and that there would still be things to smile about. Then, later that week when my dad was still in the hospital, I had a hard day coping with everything and I got another miracle. One night my brother had to scramble to help me as I fell to pieces crying uncontrollably. My hair would not go into braids for my Halloween costume, and that was apparently the thing that broke me. He calmed me down and braided my hair. He created the best braid ever! Not one hair moved out of that braid all night. That might seem like a small thing to you, but it was a big deal to me. I know my brother cannot braid like that. My Heavenly Father knew I needed some divine intervention, even if it was a small and simple thing. I needed my hair to work and my brother and I had an experience that drew us closer together during a difficult time.

The next few months were hard, but tender mercies were in no short supply. My dad was allergic to some medicine he was given and got quite sick. After his medicines got situated, the chemo made him ill. There was something every week that made things go bad. I hated to see my mother cry, but I was the one she trusted to comfort her. I think to avoid the heartache I would stay at school long after the final bell. When I was at school, I was in a different world, a world where I was not affected by cancer. I had some of the most amazing teachers that helped me through those months. I truly learned the difference teachers can make that year. If I ever needed anything, they were there for me, whether it was for a hall pass when I needed to cry in the hall, or if I just needed someone to talk to. I wished more kids at my school would have realized the amazing support we had as students. Those teachers and staff cared about us, not just our grades.

Through it all, my family grew closer together and we were enriched by the Spirit. Another one of the tender mercies Heavenly Father provided my family was my ability to understand my father. With my dad's partial tongue and his tracheotomy, it was very hard to understand him. But I could always understand him. I tell people that talking with my mouth full gave me the talent, but I always knew it came from God. My father could never understand how I understood what he said, but I always did and still do.

Eventually my dad got his feeding tube, tracheotomy, and various other medical contraptions removed and he was given a clean bill of health. My dad has been cancer-free for ten years now. I look back at that time of trial and realize that if I made it through something as hard as that, with all those mercies occurring, then I can make it now, because my Heavenly Father will help me again. This experience strengthened my testimony and my faith in ways I cannot describe. I know that those events prepared me to face more challenges in my life and helped me become the person I am today.

DETOUR THREE: SERVICE

Because Jesus Christ suffered greatly, He understands our suffering. He understands our grief. We experience hard things so that we too may have increased compassion and understanding for others."

You and I are not the only ones who experience hard times and need cheering up in our lives. Everyone—every single person with flesh and blood—experiences mortal trials and times of agony. Have you ever considered that a great way to overcome our trials, and benefit from our past trials, is to help others in their time of need?

President Dieter F. Uchtdorf said,

Often, the answer to our prayer does not come while we're on our knees but while we're on our feet serving the Lord and serving those around us. Selfless acts of service and consecration refine our spirits, remove the scales from our spiritual eyes, and open the windows of heaven. By becoming the answer to someone's prayer, we often find the answer to our own.

Service can not only benefit the lives we make a difference in but also can benefit us. We know that we feel good after service and that making another person smile is worth all the hard work, but service is a unique opportunity for the Lord to teach or show us the answers that we have been so earnestly seeking.

It is through service that not only our own trials seem less burdensome, but we also make friendships and gain experiences that last beyond this life.

Elder M. Russell Ballard taught in his April 2011 general conference talk,

Through our heartfelt kindness and service, we can make friends with those whom we serve. From these friendships come better understanding of our devotion to the gospel and a desire to learn more about us.

The love the Savior described is an active love. It is not manifested through large and heroic deeds but rather through simple acts of kindness and service.

A friend related the following story about how service touched her life: "A friend of mine had been doing more in her life to serve and be in tune with those that needed help. She was also saving up to buy a gaming system and had saved $150. She had the impression one day that she needed to send me the money. $150 was a lot of money and so she decided to send $50. The impression came again and said 'no, send $150'. So my friend said she would send it Monday. Again the impression urged her to send the money and to send it today. She sent the money and it arrived to me on Monday morning. At this time in my life I had just completed my first semester of teaching high school and did not have the funds to do much more than survive. I desperately needed to get home to see my family a state away. I needed support and I needed the encouragement my family would provide. I unfortunately had no money to my name to make the trip. Then I received the $150 in the mail. I would be able to go home. I had the intense feeling that I was loved. Not only did I have a friend who loved me, but a Heavenly Father who was aware of me and blessed me through the service of a friend. That has been one of the most touching stories of service in my life and I will always cherish that experience along with all that it teaches."

It is no understatement that tremendous things can happen through simple acts of service. The crazy thing about service is that we may never know how it will impact others, but I wish to assure you our acts, great and small, matter. My friend had a divine tender mercy where she truly came to know her Savior more and grew with love, all because a friend listened to the promptings she felt. What might be a sacrifice to us—whether it be of time, money, or physical strength—can be a miracle to those we help. Hearts, attitudes, and futures can change from a simple hello, from carrying in the groceries, or from being there to listen. Charity is a powerful thing; it can heal others and ourselves.

Matthew 25:40

"Verily I say unto you, Inasmuch as ye have done it unto one of the least of these my brethren, ye have done it unto me."

SURVEY SAYS

What is your favorite way to serve others?

"I love to randomly drop off dinner to a family, single lady, widow, or widower. It's even better to do it anonymously." - Sandy

"Making others laugh or smile." - Brian

"I like to do service projects that involve crafts. (Making blankets for children's hospital, making warm socks for the homeless, etc.) Also babysitting to let the mom and dad have some time off. Kiddos always make life happier!!!" -Rylee

"Give people gifts of sunshine! Give them something they need or give them a smile!"
- Joseph

WENDY WHITING

DETOUR FOUR: STUDY THE SCRIPTURES

Often times, it is during our hardest trials when our hearts are the most open. One thing I have found effective in my life is to study the gospel. Some say it is hard to read the scriptures every day, but I think the hard thing is remembering to read them, not the reading itself. If we make the effort to make sure we remember to read the words written in these inspired works, even if we do not fully understand them, I promise that Heavenly Father will bless us. How can I promise this? If you remember the scriptures you are remembering Him. It is promised in 3 Nephi 18:7: "And if ye do always remember me ye shall have my Spirit to be with you." The Spirit of the Holy Ghost can do marvelous things for us, especially while we are hard-pressed.

But the Comforter, which is the Holy Ghost, whom the Father will send in my name, he shall teach you all things, and bring all things to your remembrance, whatsoever I have said unto you.

Peace I leave with you, my peace I give unto you: not as the world giveth, give I unto you. Let not your heart be troubled, neither let it be afraid.

What an amazing promise the Lord gives us! If we remember Him, He will send the Holy Ghost to be with us. The Holy Ghost will teach us what we need to know about our trials. The Holy Ghost will bring to remembrance all things that will help us get through these trials amongst other things. The Holy Ghost will bring peace— real peace! What could help us more than the Holy Ghost with his many talents when we are going through such restless times?

Not only will reading the Book of Mormon help to bring the Holy Ghost into our lives, but those scriptures were written specifically for our day, so why would there not be something in there that can help? Think about it. It was not easy to write on those metal plates. Book of Mormon prophets did not have a word processor to type into and a metal engraving printer—they had to carve every syllable! Do you not think that perhaps they made sure everything they wrote down would be important to us?

Wherefore, they are of worth unto the children of men, and he that supposeth that they are not, unto them will I speak particularly, and confine the words unto mine own people; for I know that they shall be of great worth unto them in the last days; for in that day shall they understand them; wherefore, for their good have I written them.

What I love about this scripture is that not only does Nephi mention that these words are intended for us and that they will be of great worth to us, but he also says that we will understand them. Sometimes the scriptures are hard to understand, right? Why did the Savior teach in parables? So that those who had the right heart and open mind would understand the greater lesson He was trying to teach. It's the same with the scriptures—they have many lessons to teach us. If we come to them with a sincere desire for knowledge, the understanding of the verses will come to us and sometimes those verses will take on new meaning as we go through different trials.

Studying the teachings of our Savior and the gospel that He directs will help us increase the presence of the Spirit all around us as well as the blessings. It is through the Comforter and the blessings we receive from allowing him in our lives through studying that allows us to survive and makes getting through our seemingly endless woe more bearable.

SURVEY SAYS

How does studying the scriptures help you feel uplifted?

"Studying the scriptures helps me most feel uplifted when I apply the verses to myself. There have often been times when I was struggling and needed reassurance. Usually that night in my scripture reading a verse would stand out that I could insert my name and liken to myself. Through those verses, I feel my Heavenly Father's love for me and know that he is watching over me. Just knowing that He is always there for me helps me feel better." -Amy

"The examples therein give me a sense of hope. They also invite the spirit that can help us receive inspiration to assist us with the problems in our lives."- Jeremy

"Studying my scriptures helps me to broaden my view and gain an eternal perspective. Having an eternal perspective helps me to realize that all my fears and worries are small."- Laurie

"I find that when I am implementing the principles taught in the scriptures is when I feel uplifted. I can read and study but what good does it do me if I don't live what I've learned?" - Sandy

ROADBLOCK THREE: JOB LOSS

I was leaving the Institute building after a class when I got a text from my mother that said, "Dad lost his job." It was like a kick to the stomach. Two things came to my mind. First, my mother needed to learn texting etiquette because some situations really do still deserve phone calls rather than texts. Second, I thought, "What is going to happen to us?"

I was in college and living at home. I had a part-time job but it really only covered my costs to get to and from school. I also had a scholarship, but my parents still had to help me pay for a lot of my school expenses. I was virtually dependent on my parents to survive. It was amazing how the sensation of insecurity came over me. I was not insecure about myself, but about how we were going to survive. The funny thing was that I had already scheduled with my friends to go to the temple to do baptisms for the dead that night—I had just had a feeling we needed to go earlier that day. Once again, the divine evidences of God show up in our lives when we need them the most.

The temple trip was great. I felt lucky to have the opportunity to go to that place of peace. The feeling I had was that things would work out eventually. In fact, for the next many months of this anxious time, one scripture kept coming to my remembrance whenever I was reaching my breaking point. That scripture was D&C 121:7:

"My son, peace be unto thy soul; thine adversity and thine afflictions shall be but a small moment."

My dad lost his job in September. He stopped working in October. Benefits and health insurance went away January first. He was let go only months before his 20th anniversary with that company. I think the painful part of the whole situation was that though many people were losing their jobs because the economy had hit bottom, my dad lost his job because his company was doing well! They had just bought another company. The company they acquired had a worker doing the same thing my dad was doing, a worker that they could pay less money to do the same job. His company had been so amazing to him when he had cancer and now they just let him go. The situation stung a little.

At first things were fine. We knew that Heavenly Father would bless us—we all knew things would work out. Optimism was in the air that fall. It was through winter and spring that things became restless. I watched as my dad slowly started to get discouraged. We all had faith, but at times, things seemed hopeless and we would let the situation get to us. My dad submitted so many applications, and it was hard not to get discouraged. A child never wants to see their parents want to give up. It truly was hard to deal with the worry of how to survive and what was going to happen to us. I was doing hard work in school and was so incredibly stressed. Just because there was on big trial going on at home it did not mean there were not a bunch of other smaller everyday stresses. I did not always handle them well, but I just kept trying to remember: these "afflictions shall be but a small moment."

In April, I finally reached my breaking point. I talked with my dad about my feelings. I was feeling like good times were never going to come again. He told me it would be okay. He told me he felt like we were on a roller coaster and we were right at the tipping point. Things are scary in anticipation, but in a minute we would be soaring. It helped me to know my dad had not given up and that he thought things would be looking up soon. I tried to remember this and it helped. I still had rough times. I feel bad for a few of my friends who said the wrong things at the wrong time and I blew up at them. However, my friends forgave me and helped me through. Friends provided the hugs and chocolate I needed.

Finally, in May my dad was offered a job.

When I look back and think about what helped me the most, it was the gratitude my family had and the friends that comforted me. Because we had little to live off of, blessings and gratitude came in abundance. Christmas was more meaningful than ever before and was one of the best because we all gave from the heart. My grandparents helped out and odd jobs always became available. We paid tithing continuously and saw the joys along with the blessings of paying a full tithe. I never had to worry about having food because my parents had a great food storage supply and were careful. I was so grateful for my parents heeding the counsel to have a year supply. We all thought that we would need it in a disaster, not in an economic crisis. Listening to the prophets truly does bless you!

I will never forget the memories of the things my friends did for me during that time. I remember going to a friend's house and she sent me home with tons of snacks and food because she had enough and wanted to help. I learned it is important to let people serve you, because they need the service as much as you do. The blessings of heaven manifest themselves if we are but willing to receive them with an open and humble heart.

DETOUR FIVE: BE GRATEFUL

If we constantly focus on the stones in our mortal path, we will almost surely miss the beautiful flower or cool stream provided by a loving Father who outlined our journey."

God's hand is in our lives, but if we are constantly looking at what is wrong, we will never see all that is right. When my father lost his job, I noticed all the little and big things I always took for granted. I always had a roof over my head, walls to keep in the warmth, and food to eat! I was provided for in all the essential areas, so what did I have to groan about? I was so grateful for the necessities that I constantly prayed in thanksgiving.

What can gratitude truly do for us?

Gratitude unlocks the fullness of life. It turns what we have into enough, and more. It turns denial into acceptance, chaos to order, confusion to clarity. It can turn a meal into a feast, a house into a home, a stranger into a friend. Gratitude makes sense of our past, brings peace for today, and creates a vision for tomorrow.

Being in a state of gratitude makes you happy, it makes others happy, and it gives you a new perspective on all you really have. Gratitude can literally turn your life or day upside down and inside out. I do not even know if I can explain in words the amazing things that can happen when we express our thanks or act on our appreciation. In fact, the funny thing about gratitude is that it blesses you in so many ways that you have more reasons to be grateful than you did before.

D&C 78:18–19 states,

"And ye cannot bear all things now; nevertheless, be of good cheer, for I will lead you along. The kingdom is yours and the blessings thereof are yours, and the riches of eternity are yours."

"And he who receiveth all things with thankfulness shall be made glorious; and the things of this earth shall be added unto him, even an hundred fold, yea, more."

I testify that our Heavenly Father truly blesses us more when we are grateful for the things he has given us. He knows that if we are grateful, He can trust us with His blessings because we are not prideful, but humble and remember Him in all things.

I challenge you to try two things to bring more gratitude into your life and then maybe you can feel the difference gratitude can make instead of me just telling you.

First, write down on a piece of paper all the things you are grateful for. Try to fill up the whole page. I did this when I was a teenager with an index card. I wrote really small and filled one whole side. It was amazing the things I could come up with that I was truly grateful for.

Second, challenge yourself to point out everything you see as a blessing from the Lord for a day or a week. See the Lord's hand in all things. When you receive a blessing or realize something happened because the Lord loves you and is aware of you, write it down and say a prayer of gratitude.

Both of these challenges and all the blessings you receive from gratitude are summed up in this beautiful hymn:

When upon life's billows you are tempest-tossed,
When you are discouraged, thinking all is lost,
Count your many blessings; name them one by one,
And it will surprise you what the Lord has done. ...
So amid the conflict, whether great or small,
Do not be discouraged; God is over all.

Count your many blessings; angels will attend,
Help and comfort give you to your journey's end.

DETOUR SIX: HAVE HOPE AND BE POSITIVE

Some essential tools to getting around life's roadblocks would be to have hope and to remain positive. Now that being said, having hope and being positive is not easy! In my life I have seen that it is during the times I need to use hope the most that it is hardest to believe. It takes courage and true faith. As Alma said, faith is to hope for things that are not seen. So sometimes we have to believe in great outcomes even if we do not see how they could be possible. President Uchtdorf once said, "There may be times when we must make a courageous decision to hope even when everything around us contradicts this hope." I love that quote because it is a reminder that hope takes courage and oftentimes will not be the easy choice.

One way to bring back hope and positivity on a rough day is to laugh. I know when times are tough the last thing you want to do is laugh! When I was a kid my dad would try to get me to laugh my anger and sadness away. He had several sneaky tricks I could not defend myself against. I always ended up smiling and the problem never seemed to be very important anymore. As I got older, my trials were not so easily pushed over, but still nothing accomplished more positive ground than a smile. Even when my father had cancer my family found the opportunity to laugh about life and to bring up good times we had had. Elder Joseph B. Wirthlin said, "The next time you're tempted to groan, you might try to laugh instead. It will extend your life and make the lives of all those around you more enjoyable." Laughter brightens hope and through hope we can create a good attitude that will carry us through.

Hope is a powerful thing. Hope can take the darkness around us and create a barrier of light. The darkness still exists, but because of hope we will not be as influenced by it. Hope can be a powerful tool to fight the despair and find the positive education in our trials.

We learn to cultivate hope the same way we learn to walk, one step at a time. As we study the scriptures, speak with our Heavenly Father daily, commit to keep the commandments of God, like the Word of Wisdom, and to pay a full tithing, we attain hope. We grow in our ability to "abound in hope, through the power of the Holy Ghost," as we more perfectly live the gospel.

If laughing, being positive, and finding light seem too hard, pray for help and remember this statement by Elder Holland, "Fighting through darkness and despair and pleading for the light is what opened this dispensation. It is what keeps it going, and it is what will keep you going."

A positive outlook and hope are not easy, but the things in this life that are not easy that are the ones that are the most worth our hard work. Being positive and having hope can change you and your outlook on your trial. Work towards positivity—I promise the blessings are worth it.

You shape your future. Now mold it with positivity.

SURVEY SAYS

What are your favorite ways to show or grow gratitude?

"I keep a journal where I write down three ways I recognized God's hand in my life that day. I love to look back at those entries—they get me through some tough ones!" -Sandy

"The ways I show gratitude are by helping others and making cards. A nice big smile and a thank you never go unappreciated. To grow gratitude I like to think of all the many things I have to be grateful for before bed each night and during the day to thank God for all the things big and small that happen to me." -Tasha

What are some good ways to stay positive?

"Knowing that there is that light at the end of the tunnel. Always knowing that this too shall pass helps. Even though that sometimes isn't what you want to hear, it's a great reminder to hang in there." -Jennifer

"Changing my mindset helps me to be positive. I focus on being grateful for the good things in my life. When I am grateful, I am more positive. It is easier to see the good around me. It is also helpful for me to be around positive people. If I am being negative, I avoid those around me who are more likely to speak negatively. It is easy to be negative when others around me are. Sometimes you have to distance yourself from that." -Amy

ROADBLOCK FOUR: ANXIETY CRASH

"Be not afraid, only believe." —Mark 5:36

"Fear not: for they that be with us are more than they that be with them." —2 Kings 6:16

Fear is a dangerous thing. Fear can cause excess stress, change our habits, and essentially alter who we are or might become. I had an experience where several people told me to simply stop fearing. Anxiety cannot just turn off like a flip of a switch. People will say things to you about how enough is enough or how it is silly to fear something so long after a traumatic event. The truth is that our bodies create fear as a defense mechanism. Mentally I knew the fear was dumb, but my fear was physical and emotional. Our bodies have a reaction system where they create fear when they recognize a dangerous situation. Simply not being afraid just because I didn't want to be was not an option, even though I wanted it so badly.

I was involved in two car accidents within a few months of each other. In both cases my car was completely stopped and there was nothing I could have done to have changed the result. My body was in pain both physically and emotionally. In one of the crashes I basically sat there and waited to be hit. Psychologically those accidents sent me into a whirlwind. I had a panic attack every time I got in my car. I felt like I lost all control over what was happening to me every time I got out on the road. I did not realize at first that this is what was happening, but even when I did, I just thought that time would cure the problem.

Unfortunately, my body was so upset and paranoid about the situation that I developed a digestive condition. I would get very sick right after eating or I would have stomach pains. I grew more and more upset because I did not understand what was going on and why I could not eat regular foods. I was down to eating a specific cereal, bread, and salad. I finally went to the doctor for tests and they didn't find anything, except that now I was lacking a nutrient or two because I wasn't eating.

Though I felt alone and afraid many times because I did not understand how to heal myself, I knew my Father in Heaven watched out for me. My mother just happened to flip channels to a program about this digestive issue that could not be proved by any test but by ruling out everything else. I watched a recording of the show later and the lady who had been diagnosed described my daily problems almost perfectly. I talked to my doctor and we developed a plan. I started eating the right type of foods my body needed and avoided ones that my body would not respond well to. Slowly I wasn't as sick anymore. The ailment that I was diagnosed with can be worsened or caused by anxiety, so I knew that if I wanted to be healthy and normal again I had to admit that I could not handle my fear and anxiety alone anymore.

I went to see a counselor and talked to her about my fears of being in another accident. I learned so much from those sessions. I learned that I was so anxious because my body was trying to defend itself against situations where it felt it did not have control. I feared driving, which I had once loved, because I never knew when a car would just hit me. There are ways to restore control and to bring peace back in our lives. The big lesson I learned was that sometimes we have to seek help or take seemingly scary steps in order for Heavenly Father to reward us with a blessing. It did not take me many sessions to regain a level of peace where I knew I could take on my fears. However, it is important to point out that how much help each person needs is different and I continued to struggle, I just knew I had the right tools I needed to face this battle because I was listening to the Spirit.

Life did not get easy after that, but I knew I could handle it. I practiced the things my counselor taught me and was grateful for the blessing of peace and reassurance God gave me. Soon after this, though, my place of employment closed. I got upset about not finding a job. I accepted a job eventually, but it was more because I wanted a job than because it was the right job. I was miserable again and I started to let my fears back in. Sometime not too much later, I realized I had let myself get to that point of depression and anxiety again. I had the control to live the life I wanted and I knew that God would help me if I followed His promptings this time.

I tried to more earnestly seek God's will and go after the dreams and interests that would truly make me happy. God gave me my talents, so I thought I should probably find a way to use them. I found a job when I needed it most by reaching out to those around me. I started a certificate program for a career I never thought was possible, and I eventually regained a stable environment for the first time in a year. God had a plan for me and still has more of a plan for me that I do not know about yet. Sometimes we have to take the stony path to get to the beautiful garden.

Through this whole journey, though it was rough and painful, I learned I can do hard things. We really can go after our dreams. God wants us to seek out those righteous dreams. We have unique talents that He gave us; He knows how we can best use them. I never would have thought that I would be on the path that I am now, but now I know that I first had to fall to learn how to be who I really am. God is always helping us see the potential we have.

DETOUR SEVEN: SEEK HELP

Had I not received help from a professional counselor, I would not have achieved the results I did in my battle with anxiety. I still have anxiety problems when I am struggling with things or am stressed more than what is needful, but because of my counselor, I learned skills and tricks I can use on my own now. She also provided counsel and help I could not have received from a friend.

I also want to put forth the idea that sometimes when we battle depression, anxiety, and other emotional disorders, we might not be chemically balanced. We might be having more than a bad month or year. I have had times where naturally, and sometimes with medications, I was not balanced hormonally and I would gravitate to despair so quickly I didn't realize I was doing it. I thought my life must really be a huge mess that these feelings existed inside of me. Many people have imbalances in their bodies and need medication to balance out these problems. Others might have medications that are too strong or create imbalances. When you are considering whether these types of imbalances are occurring in your life, always talk to a doctor. We are not educated enough often times to make decisions regarding medications. Doctors and pharmacists know the potential dangers and side effects of medications and can help you find this balance over time. Never take these matters into your own hands because they can have fatal or dangerous results.

Overall, we have to be willing to seek help for our problems. Jeffrey R. Holland said in general conference in October 2013,

"If you had appendicitis, God would expect you to seek a priesthood blessing and get the best medical care available. So too with emotional disorders. Our Father in Heaven expects us to use all of the marvelous gifts He has provided in this glorious dispensation."

There comes a time when we have to realize that others have talents that can help us more than we can help ourselves. Heavenly Father gave us all unique talents and gifts so that we can work together and have everything that we need. But how can we access all of these blessings and opportunities if we do not ask or seek? There are people in your life and in your community that Heavenly Father has sent there for you. You might find this hard to believe, but I have seen this too many times not to know that it is true. I have had friends in my life that came at such an opportune time with their unique talent to help me in a particular situation. For example, the counselor I went to had unique qualities that helped me personally.

How can we access these people and their talents? Search. Ponder. Pray. Search for the type of help you need and see who is available and who would help you best. Ponder on your options and really learn about them. Then pray about your findings and thoughts. I prayed about whom to see, and through listening and being worthy of the Spirit, I was able to decide that I needed to see a counselor, that I could go, and that there was a counselor that was right for me. When I got to her office, I got a further witness that I was in the right place, because I had included the Spirit in my process.

In the same talk referenced above, Jeffrey R. Holland reiterates something we all need to remember:

"So how do you best respond when mental or emotional challenges confront you or those you love? Above all, never lose faith in your Father in Heaven, who loves you more than you can comprehend. ... Never, ever doubt that, and never harden your heart."

Always seek the help of your Heavenly Father. You can reach out to your parents, to your friends, your church leaders, your bishop, and many more. But always remember that no matter what, your Father in Heaven is there for you. He is aware of you. He is crying with you and loves you unconditionally. He might have to draw away from you if you choose not to be worthy of His Spirit, but he is always aware of you and will always hear and answer your prayers. He might not answer immediately, and He might not give you the answer you want, but He knows the best answer even though you might not ever be able to imagine what that answer is. Oftentimes, when our answer is no or is different from what we expect, it is because a greater blessing is coming if we but follow the right path.

DETOUR EIGHT: PRAY OFTEN AND EARNESTLY

First of all, understand that your Father in Heaven loves you and He hears your prayers. "Your Father in Heaven knows your name and your circumstance. He hears your prayers. He knows your hopes and dreams, including your fears and frustrations. And He knows what you can become through faith in Him." I testify, without a doubt in my mind, that He knows each and every one of us personally. He knows what is in store for us and He wants so much to help us if we just ask Him and come unto Him.

Pay attention to the following quote. What does it teach us about Heavenly Father's character?

Even if you cannot always see that silver lining on your clouds, God can, for He is the source of the light you seek. He does love you, He knows your fears. He hears your prayers. He is your Heavenly Father, and surely He matches with His own the tears His children shed.

Often times we think of God as a powerful ruler who, if we pray incorrectly, will chastise us and plague our lives. This is not the case at all. He wants us to come to Him. Christ repeats that over and over again in the scriptures: "Come unto me." He is upset when we are not happy. Our Heavenly Father wants to bless us and wants to show us all the beauties this life has to offer us, but He cannot do that unless we seek Him.

In an Institute class, I was given a challenge to have a great prayer—a prayer where you truly communicate with your Heavenly Father and learn from Him what you need in your life. This prayer required preparation. Our class made a list of what would help us to be able to even have such a magnificent prayer. Some of the things we decided we needed to do were pray for a great prayer, pray for the Spirit and live worthy of it, read the scriptures, and read our patriarchal blessings.

I prepared for this prayer for a few days and planned on going to the temple on Friday to pray. On Thursday night a miracle occurred. My parents had also decided they were going to go to the temple. I asked if I could join them and my dad got an idea. My dad went to the computer to see if he could prepare any family names fast enough for us to take them to the temple to have their work done. My mother's family is a particularly hard line to do work for because of some of their culture and the lack of records kept in the family. That Thursday night my dad found information that he had never been able to locate before and thus was able to have several names ready for Friday morning. I had never been baptized for my own relatives. I was tremendously excited.

Friday morning I was baptized for several of my ancestors and spent a wonderful morning in the temple with my family. I went outside and sat among the beautiful temple grounds. I prayed. I received answers and assurances I had been longing for. My soul truly had sunshine radiating from it. Not only had I prayed to my Heavenly Father, but I communicated with Him and really sought to listen for answers. Sometimes we do not take enough care and time to truly listen to what our Father in Heaven wants to tell us, even if it is the answer we are earnestly asking for. We must listen too. That experience taught me how important prayer is and that it is not just a ritual, but a great opportunity to become closer to our Heavenly Father who loves us and truly wants us to ask and receive blessings.

We must come to Him with an open heart and mind, along with the humility to listen.

SURVEY SAYS

Where is a good place to go to feel the Spirit and to receive answers?

"The temple would always be my first choice if I wanted a change of location where I could really feel the Spirit to receive answers. I feel, though, that even when I can't make it to the temple, my home is its own kind of temple. I can find a quiet time when I'm alone and remove all distractions. My bedroom is usually that sanctuary for me where I feel like I can talk to my Heavenly Father and feel His Spirit guide me. For me, nature is also a place where I can feel the Spirit and feel guidance. I know it isn't always easy to get away, but I have felt close to the Spirit just sitting out on the porch swing at a cabin. I feel like nature, and being away from distractions, can allow you to better hear the spirit." - Amy

"Most of my inspiration has come while pondering and praying in my room. What's important is to be somewhere where we can get away from the distractions of the world, where we can be in the present moment. That is where most of my inspiration has come, in my experience." - Jeremy

"I would say the temple, but most often I find that going for a walk or drive alone with no distractions is a good way for me to tune in to the thoughts and impressions I may be receiving that I wouldn't notice with all the commotion of life." - Sandy

NEVER GIVE UP

Don't give up. Keep going when it seems too hard, because the Lord will not give you trials you are not able to bear. Keep your faith to the end and you will be a conqueror and a survivor. Sometimes when situations are so tough, all we can do is just make it one more day, and at times that is all the Lord asks of us.

President Uchtdorf said in his October 2013 general conference address,

"Our destiny is not determined by the number of times we stumble but by the number of times we rise up, dust ourselves off, and move forward."

I have been afraid of failure or messing up the Lord's plan for me. Many times, especially as a young adult, I have wondered if I was making the wrong decision. Sometimes we make decisions ten times bigger in our heads than what they really are. For example, in reality, it does not matter what shirt we wear each day, but yet some days as we get dressed we act like it will have eternal consequences if we wear the green shirt and not the blue one. Yes, this is a silly example, but we really do put too much weight on small choices at times because they seem so big in that moment. Perhaps in some instances we also do not give ourselves enough credit to make the right decision. But if we are worthy of having the Spirit with us, worthy of the covenants we make, and worthy to be at the temple, then we cannot mess up His plan. President Howard W. Hunter reinforced this idea when he said,

"If our lives and our faith are centered upon Jesus Christ and His restored gospel, nothing can ever go permanently wrong."

That quote has given me so much comfort. We each have our own way of receiving revelation, but often when I am worried about messing up the Lord's plan, or my life in general, I remember this quote and that if I am worthy to go to the Lord's house, then I will have His guidance when I need it. He will direct our paths. He will stop us when we need stopping and push us when we need pushing.

Right after I graduated college I didn't know what I wanted to do. I applied for jobs like crazy. I applied for a graduate program. I tried to move. To all of those attempts the Lord would very clearly throw a brick wall in my path or huge gaping Grand Canyon. Needless to say, I knew very well that those were not the paths the Lord wanted. I had a harder time figuring out the "right" path and I cannot tell you I have even figured it out yet. But I can tell you that when paths or decisions Heavenly Father wanted me to take for sure came along, I felt such peace and such happiness that it was worth the wait. Sometimes the perfect path for us is a path we cannot see nor predict let alone even fathom in our wildest dreams.

My freshman year of high school I was put into a class that was my absolute last choice for an elective. I was bummed when I had to go to journalism class, because although I did well in English class, I was no writer. On the first day of school I learned that due to cut backs our journalism class would be thrown into newspaper class after a few weeks of learning more about the writing process. I wanted to leave that class immediately! However, after some thought, I decided I was going to give it a month and if it did not work out I would switch classes. I really put a good effort into the class. I wrote and tried to implement the new techniques I was learning. It came time to switch over to newspaper and I decided I liked the class, but I told my teacher that I just wanted to be a photographer. A week or so after we submitted the papers of what we would like our assignments to be, I got asked to stay after class. My teacher told me that I was talented and was among the better writers in the class. He challenged me to not give up, to be a writer, and to keep trying to improve.

I loved my newspaper experience. I tried my best to improve my writing, and when I saw my work in print inside a newspaper I was so happy. At the end of the semester, my teacher left the school to pursue a principal job and as I left one day he stopped me and made me promise I would continue writing. He helped me to believe in my skills and pushed me to improve.

Because of that experience, I made more goals and continued to improve my writing skills. I went on to get my bachelor's degree in English, where I studied and learned so much about writing. I do not profess to be a great writer, because there is always room for improvement; but from sticking to it and not giving up, I gained one of my favorite talents that has turned into a passion. Sure, there are days when I do not seem to be progressing and improving. But those days are there to remind me that these tasks are not easy but still worth it in the end. Anything that will bring us true eternal happiness is worth the pains of improving.

SURVEY SAYS

If you could give any advice to teens that are going through what we have been through, what would it be?

"I would let them know to never forget that their Heavenly Father loves them and is with them. Even when they feel alone, or like their prayers aren't being answered, they really are being watched over and guided. They can always pray sincerely and receive the confirmation that their Father loves them. Life will seem very hard, even to the point of feeling like it will never get better, but with the right kind of help and seeking for heavenly guidance they can make it through the trials. Each one of us is given trials, but we are never given more than we can handle. Just remember that Heavenly Father has allowed you to have those trials with the knowledge that you can make it through." -Amy

"Smile often and remember that you are never alone, never forgotten and you matter immensely. You have been sent to Earth at this time for a reason; you matter! Just keep going!" - Laurie

"Oh man. Being a teenager was rough. I remember when I was a teenager and people telling me that your 20s are so much better, and your 30s are even better than that, and so on. I didn't believe it. But now that I'm in my 20s I know they were right. Being a teenager is so hard. I would tell teenagers today that no matter how they feel, no matter what anyone tells them, I promise them they are amazing individuals and super cool people and they deserve their own self love because they are really worth it. When other kids put you down it's because they are feeling badly about themselves. So love yourself and love others. And when you're feeling down, no matter how down you feel, it will get better. They say it does and truly it does. Whenever I would get mad or sad about something silly, I would tell myself, "This is the one chance you have to be happy in this moment! And if you're not happy now you won't get the chance to be happy in this moment again." It was good motivation. I know some things aren't silly. That's different. Do your best to sit down, put your emotions aside and think about it logically. Talking with a good friend can help you get perspective. Though I also have to say I had some bad apple type friends as a teen so maybe get your parents' perspective too." - Tasha

"I would tell them that it gets better. It may seem like it never will, but it will, in time. We learn, grow, and gain strength from our challenges, whatever they may be. Lean on Him, turn to Him and do all you can to be like Him, but keep in mind that you're human and perfection is an eternal progression." Sandy

CONCLUSION

Good things can come from trials.

Learning to endure times of disappointment, suffering, and sorrow is part of our on-the-job training. These experiences, while often difficult to bear at the time, are precisely the kinds of experiences that stretch our understanding, build our character, and increase our compassion for others.

Life is hard sometimes, and though that will never change, I promise you happy times can come again. Your results are dependent upon you. You can take your experiences and act: build your character, gain compassion for others, and mold something positive out of your negatives. However, if you choose to do nothing and be idle, you will feel that hunger you cannot calm with anything the world has to offer. It simply will not work. I earnestly pray you never let your heart and soul get to that dark place. There is always hope, even if you are not able to see how life will play out positively. I promise if you humbly seek your Heavenly Father, He will come to you. You will have to accept His plan and that might not always be easy, but His way is what is best for you and He will never ever leave you comfortless. He promises us that!

John 14:18

"I will not leave you comfortless: I will come to you."

That was the first scripture that I truly remember crying over and being so truly touched by. It is true and such a great promise. I can testify of that scripture's truth!

I also suggest going to the temple. Even if you cannot regularly do temple work inside, at least be on the temple grounds. There have been many sorrowful days I have spent at the temple where I have been uplifted. Sometimes the power from the temple allowed me to have an hour of peace to make it one more day, but other times I received an answer or peace that changed my life. No matter what inspiration came or how great of an impact a temple trip had, each and every time I stepped on those sacred grounds I was embraced by hope and a love only the Savior and our Father in Heaven can give to us on this earth. The temple and the covenants we make there are powerful. I like to think each time we go to His temple or perform those sacred ordinances for his other children we get points towards our blessings. Now this does not translate into reality, but I think each time we go to the temple we are blessed because we are showing our gratitude, humility, and our Christlike love for our brothers and sisters on the other side of the veil. Those reasons and many more are why we get so immensely blessed by going to the House of the Lord. So if nothing else seems to be working, at least spend time at His holy house, where peace and miracles can be found.

I hope that something in this book has touched your heart. Our Creator has a great plan of happiness and that included coming to this world to be tested. I do not really like tests and I bet you have come along some that have been real roadblocks too. The amazing thing is that every time we are blocked there is not a stop sign; there is a detour sign. He gives us ways around or through these problems if we are willing to look for them and come unto him to learn how to best get through them. We can get through them by being bitter and turning to what the world or those jerks in high school say is the right way, but it will not be a way of light nor peace. I can testify that what I have said is true because I have personally lived it. I have cried and prayed on my knees in what was true agony of my soul. I saw no happily ever after and I saw no peace in sight. My Heavenly Father came to me in all of my times of need. He calmed my fears and filled my heart with peace. My troubles never went away instantly. But all those times I was crying on my floor, He came to me with His love enveloping me. He can do the same for you. Have patience with your situation and yourself. Never give up on Him or on yourself. Give your Heavenly Father the opportunity to show His love for you, by coming unto him and learning of him.

WORKS CITED

Ballard, M. Russell. "Finding Joy Through Loving Service." The Ensign. May 2011.

Beattie, Melody. Quoteland.com. 1997-2001. http://www.quoteland.com/topic/Gratitude-Quotes/252/?pg=1 (accessed 2011).

Eyring, Henry B. "True Friends." Ensign. May 2002.

Holland, Jeffrey R. "High Priest of Good Things to Come." The Ensign. November 1999.

Hunter, Howard W. "Fear Not, Little Flock." BYU Devotional. March 1989, 1989.

Mendenhall, Laurie, interview by Wendy Whiting. (November 1, 2014).

Monson, Thomas S. "The Divine Gift of Gratitude." The Ensign. November 2010.

Uchtdorf, Dieter F. "The Infinite Power of Hope." The Ensign. November 2008.

Uchtdorf, Dieter F. "Waiting on the Road to Damascus ." Ensign. May 2011.

Uchtdorf, Dieter. "You Can Do It Now!" October 2013.

Various, interview by Survery. Detour from Darkness (October 1-15, 2014).

Wirthlin, Joseph B. "Come What May, and Love It." The Ensign. November 2008.

Teachings of the Presidents of the Church: Spencer W. Kimball[2006], 82.

Holland, Jeffrey R. Created For Greater Things. Salt Lake City: Deseret Book Company, 2011. Pg 5.

Monson, Thomas S. "An Attitude of Gratitude." Ensign. May 2000.

Holland, Jeffrey R. "Like a Broken Vessel." Ensign. November 2013.

ABOUT THE AUTHOR

Wendy Whiting grew up in the sweltering heat of Phoenix, Arizona. She spent most of her childhood outside with her older brothers, getting into mischief and learning to play sports without getting a burn from the pavement. Wendy learned a love of reading and writing at a young age and continued her education at Arizona State University, where she graduated with a bachelor's degree in English.

Made in the USA
Las Vegas, NV
04 January 2025

15825639R00038